HOW TO ANALYSE YOUR CHILD'S HANDWRITING AND DRAWINGS

PATRICIA MARNE

D0063955

An OPTIMA book

First published in 1991 by
Macdonald Optima, a division of
Macdonald & Co. (Publishers) Ltd

A member of Maxwell Macmillan Publishing Corporation

British Library Cataloguing in Publication Data

Marne, Patricia
    Understanding your child's writing and drawings.
    I. Title
    155.2083

    ISBN 0-356-20127-9

Macdonald & Co (Publishers) Ltd
165 Great Dover St
London
SE1 4YA

Typeset in Century Schoolbook by
Leaper & Gard Ltd, Bristol, England
Printed and bound in Great Britain by
The Guernsey Press Co. Ltd, Guernsey, Channel Islands

CONTENTS

ABOUT THE AUTHOR

Patricia Marne is a graphologist, founder member and Chairwoman of the Graphologist Society. As a leading expert in her field, she specialises in personnel selection and crime. Patricia Marne has published many articles on graphology, plus several books, notably *Teach Yourself Graphology* (Hodder 1980), *The Criminal Hand* (Sphere 1991) and *How to Analyse Your Handwriting* (Optima, 1991).

PREFACE

This book gives you an opportunity to study the hidden personality that lies behind your child's handwriting or drawings. The significance of these scribbles can provide an insight into understanding your child a little better. They reveal clues to his subconscious mind and bring to light any tiny lurking fears, apprehensions, or anxieties that may be worrying him.

The symbolism that emerges in both handwriting and drawings often shows friction within the family or school, sibling rivalry and even stress. Once these conflicts are detected at an early stage they can be dealt with swiftly so that the child can be helped with his difficulties.

ANALYSING CHILDREN'S HANDWRITING

Before studying children's handwriting for analysis it is necessary to know something of the basic rules of graphology, for it is essential that the elementary guidelines are known. The following chapters therefore give you a brief outline of what to look for and the meaning of the samples shown.

At the outset, however, it must be emphasised that it is necessary to know the age, sex and nationality of the writer before attempting an analysis: the age because some people are still young at 70, others old at 20; the sex because everyone has characteristics of both sexes in their make-up; while nationality will provide clues to where the child was taught to write, as there may be national characteristics to be taken into consideration.

1
INFLUENCES ON HANDWRITING

Writing is 'brain writing', i.e. it is a form of expression that is affected by all sorts of outside influences on the personality.

The form of an individual's handwriting is the result of three interacting impulses – motor, formative and spatial – all originating from the brain.

- The brain sends a message to the hand when you write. This is the motor impulse; it is a normal reflex action, and demonstrates the ability to form letters.
- The formative impulse is the writer's individual style of writing. As a result of all sorts of influences this will cause the handwriting to deviate from a 'copybook' style, so that it is truly the writer's own style.
- The spatial impulse is the writer's use of space, lines, margins, etc. Again, various influences will affect how he or she deals with them and makes use of them.

As a child matures, so should the handwriting; he or she will adopt his or her own special style of script, such that no two styles of handwriting are the same – even identical twins have different handwriting. The handwriting may certainly change with illness and trauma, age and maturity, but the fundamental characteristics are with us for life.

Education authorities in this country have never been bothered by the style of handwriting taught in schools. There have been attempts to improve or simplify it – the Marion Richardson method in the 1930s, for example – but they have never been widespread. Because we do not have one particular method of writing, it is therefore allowed to be more or less individualistic. This is in contrast to the USA, where the immature Palmer style is adopted. The teaching of handwriting in this country, however, is left to the teacher and his or her individual idiosyncracies.

Many other aspects of a child's life and upbringing will affect the style of handwriting they adopt, though. Before examining the details of handwriting style it would therefore be useful to see what some of these influences might be.

HOME

Home, family, friends and school make up the child's world; these are the areas where the child's personality is developed. But the most important influence on a child is the cultural, environmental and psychological milieu of the home; what happens to a child from the age of a few weeks to five years moulds its character for life. For example, maladjusted children who grow up neurotic often have neurotic parents; children who live in an environment where violence is the norm often become hostile and aggressive, or withdraw into themselves; children who live within a rigid family structure may grow up with a fear of expressing their true thoughts and feelings, and so become introverted. It is thus a mistake for parents to believe that their attitudes towards their partners, relatives and friends go unnoticed by their children. The parents might think that the child is too young to understand, but, invariably, this is not the case; children pick up the personal likes and dislikes, habits and attitudes, of the adults around them. Indeed, this is the very reason why fears and anxieties can be handed down and can take root at a very early age in children.

Competitiveness in a family can be a good thing, but when carried to extremes it can breed anxiety in a highly sensitive child. In particular, sibling rivalry can be very intense in some families; if one child is clever and the other one not, this can result in the less intelligent child refusing to assert himself and resigning himself to being a failure, perhaps avoiding any sort of decision-making.

One area of family life, in particular, that breeds rebellion in children – especially teenagers – is where there is a strong repressive religious background. This narrow spiritual outlook can smother any individuality the child may have, and may be a great source of irritation to young adults, who find the harsh and often rigidly held views and opinions of their parents hard to tolerate. It should then be no surprise that they try to break loose. Undercurrents like this can breed hostility and friction within the family, and can turn to aggression when the child sets out to flout the repressive atmosphere, or takes out his resentment in acts of violence. The child who lives under these conditions is a hostage to rebellion.

Sometimes this hostility and rebellion can evidence itself in anti-social behaviour on the part of the child, shoplifting being a classic example. And it is a mistake to believe that such behaviour only emanates from working-class homes; it can equally well happen in middle-class homes and in the upper strata of society if the predisposing factors are there in the first place. Where there is turmoil in the home, such disturbances in children emerge as a way of coping.

Many children have these sorts of problems. And although parents and teachers may be excellent at looking after the child's welfare, if they are unskilled in child guidance, they cannot be expected to recognise and understand the basis for these problems. They may suspect something is not quite right, but fail to spot the area of conflict. This is where graphology can be such a help; when the signs of stress or anxiety surface in the handwriting, graphology can detect them. Appropriate steps can then be taken to prevent the problem from developing, or specialised help sought so that it doesn't remain with the child for life.

CLASS

In general, middle-class children have many more opportunities to expand and express their personalities in more creative ways than the lower-income-group child. Reading, writing, painting and creative outlets are more readily available, and all help to avoid neurotic tendencies developing.

By involving children in activities where they are mixing socially in the community – taking them to museums, theatres, dancing classes, the ballet, music lessons, etc. – middle-class parents can provide a wide window on the world that the poorer child, whose parents don't have the money or time, misses out on. Such children can usually only play in the street or playground, where they are often left to their own devices and the influence of perhaps undesirable playmates. When a child lacks an identity within the family or community he may lash out at society, hitting out to get rid of frustration he is not equipped to handle in a more positive manner. He strikes back to compensate for his feelings of inadequacy, even though he doesn't always realise it.

On a more practical level, if space is available for each individual child to read, study and listen or write in, he is going to be way ahead of the child who may have to share a living room with parents, siblings and even other relations. Certainly children who are read to, and have their writing taken an interest in by parents will usually write with better speed and accuracy than children who are left to rely only on a teacher.

MOTIVATION

Children who appear dull and disinterested in class may not have been motivated by teacher or parent. This can lead to frustration and poor school-work.

But equally, disturbances in the home or schoolroom are often caused by the child seeking attention; he may be intelligent but unable to express his thoughts and feelings, and so vents his frustration in disruptive behaviour. Good motivation can act as a spur in this situation, especially if the child has a sense of achievement, a sense of pride, once a goal has been attained.

Similarly children who are perhaps cleverer than their peers in class, and who show originality in their handwriting, perhaps with features that are recognisably more sophisticated, may have to linger behind other children who are not so mature. This can result in boredom setting in, with the prospect of frustration, and disruptive behaviour emerges as a means of fighting that boredom. Usually such children are more active outside school, where they are able to develop their interests and compensate by mixing with older children.

STRESS

Children as well as adults suffer from stress. Once one is aware of a child's stress level they can then be given assistance to overcome their difficulties; for example, stress can be released by channelling energies into games, sports and activities that give pleasure and keep the child occupied and happy. However, it is also important to ensure that the child isn't over-motivated; children are not able to concentrate for long periods at a time, and so need realistic goals to aim for.

BATTERED CHILDREN

It is a sad fact that many children who have been treated badly by their parents or by other adults grow up to become child abusers or batterers themselves. There is therefore a twofold urgency in detecting child battering or abuse. Children themselves are often the only reliable sources of information about their abuse by adults, but unfortunately, being children, they aren't always believed by other adults.

An analysis of an abused child's handwriting can be very helpful in this context. Violence is seen in angles, fluctuating pressure and pointed strokes, while sexual abuse is often seen in extra large letters, disconnected and wide, with more pressure being applied to especially 'motive' words such as 'God', 'mother', 'father'. When violently abused children are asked to write a little story they may make it aggressive and hostile, with many characters using brutality as a means of interest.

MOTHER INFLUENCE

If there is a strong mother influence on a child in its early formative years – particularly if the child is without a father – this will have a profound affect on the child's personality. This will tend to be particularly apparent in a male child, as the combination of factors may well be responsible for subsequent difficulties in maintaining satisfactory or normal relationships with the opposite sex. Future potential problems of this sort can often be identified from an examination of the child's handwriting.

Similarly, an analysis of handwriting at around the age of 10 can often reveal possible emotional and sexual preferences – for example, homosexuality. It must be emphasised, however, that such analysis will point to latent homosexuality, which may or may not develop as the child grows up.

LEFT HANDEDNESS

No left-handed child should ever be made to write with his right hand, as this can cause nervousness. For example, King George VI was made to write with his right hand by his father, even though he was left handed. He also suffered from a stutter, so it is to be wondered how much the adoption of another hand to write with went against his natural inclinations and added to his problems.

It doesn't matter which hand the child holds the pen in, as long as he is happy and comfortable.

CAREER CHOICES

Although graphology can detect creative talents – music or drawing, for example – and can reveal many other facets of a child's character, handwriting should not be analysed for career guidance before the age of 11 or 12. Signposts to certain subject preferences can be seen earlier, but not with any guarantee of certainty.

2
PRACTICAL DETAILS

Confident, well spaced and well-formed writing, with medium pressure and a right slant, usually shows the child who is loved, cared for, confident. But graphology can reveal so much more – originality, creativity, a talent for drama or detail, as well as taking into consideration the mental, social and emotional features of the handwriting and overall balance of the script.

Where does one start? What sort of examples of hand-writing should be examined? And what can be done to help a child with their handwriting? The following are some important practical points to bear in mind:

- Writing on unlined paper is good for disciplining the eye.
- Asking a child to write a little story can work wonders for his self-confidence, and can help him or her to become familiar with the printed word.
- Practising their names gives children a feeling of self-importance.
- Neat and tidy writing is frequently a sign of compulsiveness rather than intelligence. Teachers often award high marks to perfect-looking legible handwriting, yet a more erratic and untidy scrawl may reveal more originality and mental ability. Children who are under pressure to do well may produce a copybook script which is legible and neat but devoid of character, whilst the more alert and creative child will have a hasty scrawl.
- Letters that are reversed show a poor focus of attention, a persistent feature of this particular trait being a reversed b and d. This indicates that the child is easily

bored, finds it hard to concentrate and is possibly over-active.

- Look for the letter o that has one or more circles round it, and heavy pressure; in so doing the writer some-times almost obliterates the letter. This can denote compulsiveness and a tendency for the child continu-ally to cover up mistakes for fear of punishment.
- Heavy full stops tell of apprehension about being criticised.
- Stacking – words that are written underneath one another, with large white spaces between them – demonstrates insecurity and unhappiness with the environment; the child could be fearful of a teacher or a member of the family who he feels is threatening his security. Such children occasionally live in a fantasy world, and will withdraw into themselves when they can't cope. Stacking is often seen in the handwriting of children who are living in an adopted country and who feel out of place.
- Connected writing shows the ability to co-operate and communicate with others. Disconnected writing not only indicates reserve and independence; it can also reveal original or creative thinking, the writer preferring to use his own ideas, and disinclined to follow the crowd.
- Large spaces between the words signify caution, an organising ability and a tendency to remain aloof. Small spaces between words show a need for com-munication.
- Extremely wide spaces indicate a fear of becoming too involved with people; psychologically or environ-mentally the writer may find it hard to communicate.
- Too narrow spaces, such that the words are crowded, shows insecurity and a strong need for human contact. The writer frequently acts with impulsiveness.
- Lines that are muddled, each one tangling with another zone, shows bad judgment, a lack of object-ivity and difficulty in assessing situations clearly.
- Enrolling (rolled round) on the lower loop can be an

indication that too much emphasis is placed on the physical instincts; there may be a preoccupation with sex.

- Heavy or thick i dots may show a sensitivity to criticism.
- Crossing out and going over letters is a sign of anxiety and stress; the child may be nervous and fearful of making mistakes.
- Over-controlled writing that is stiff and inflexible shows a compulsion neurosis.
- Latent aggressive tendencies can manifest themselves in firm angles, spiky strokes and triangles in the t and g.
- Where there are few rounded strokes in the script and the t bar crossing is pointed, this reveals the child who refuses to conform, who is aggressive and unco-operative; possibly they are suffering from anxiety, leading to tension which needs release.
- Deaf children write better than children who don't have hearing problems, simply because they often get more attention.
- Children who are dyslexic are quite often creative, but frustrated; this frustration can turn to aggression when their problem isn't detected.

CAPITAL I

This personal pronoun is significant in handwriting analysis and should always be given special consideration. Like the signature, it is an ego sign and the way it is dealt with conveys quite a lot about the writer's feelings towards self.

- The tiny minute capital I can reveal an inferiority complex.
- The exaggerated I, perhaps enrolled or elaborated, may show feelings of insecurity, compensated for by a desire for attention and showing off.
- When a weak I is seen it denotes either that the identity is not particularly dominant, and the child is

unable to project their personality, or that there could be a physical weakness.

- A capital I that leans to the left, while the rest of the script is right slanted or upright, shows a guilt complex, emotional problems, and a possible difficulty in expressing ideas or firm resolve.
- A child who feels alientated from his family may separate his capital I from the rest of his words. Very often the writing will have a left slant.

These subconscious thoughts are projected on to paper as symbolic graphic forms that can be analysed; Carl Jung, the celebrated Swiss psychologist, called them 'abstract thoughts condensed into an image'.

THE SIGNATURE

Like the I, the signature is also an ego symbol. It is the most important thing a person can write. Children are taught their name before attempting anything else, practising it over and over again so that it becomes familiar and the child enjoys seeing it in print. 'I can write my name' they say, with pride.

As the child gets older the signature will therefore be far more mature than the rest of the writing. This is because he is in a small way projecting an image of himself on to paper, and as he becomes more mature, this image is going to represent the way he wants the world to see him.

It is possible to detect anxiety in a child's signature at an early age. Some research has been done on this in the USA; for example, it was found that a cross drawn underneath the signature was often placed there by children who had been ill treated.

TEENAGE WRITING

In teenage writing the co-ordination and speed, rhythm and size, are factors that are important when assessing intelligence and potential. Are they erratic or smooth, fast or slow, firm and confident or undulating and irregular?

Boys and girls between the ages of 13 and 16 will show many changes in their handwriting, reflecting their emerging emotional feelings. There will be sudden spurts of pressure, varying slants, exaggeration of capital letters – all indications and signs of their changing emotions. These are common factors, and significant, and must be taken into consideration from as many samples as possible.

Teenage writing that has unexpected spurts of pressure can indicate a writer who is avoiding stressful situations by a 'flight' response from his problems; when this occurs in the handwriting of 14 or 15 year olds it should only last for a short period of time. Illegible signature in teenage writing may reveal confusion about the sexual role they are expected to follow; by concealing their name, they are protecting themselves from the outside world which they feel is hostile. This 'wrapping up' of their signature is usually found in the 14–16 age group.

3
THE THREE ZONES

There are three basic zones of handwriting, and all handwriting analysis starts with an examination of these three zones.

- The upper zone contains the ascenders of the letters.
- The middle zone contains the main body of the letters.
- The lower zone contains the descenders of the letters.

The upper zone reveals the intellect, ethics and moral values of the individual. The middle zone expresses the area between the spiritual (upper) zone and the materialistic (lower) zone; it shows how the writer copes with everyday matters, and demonstrates his or her social attitude. The lower zone indicates the sexual, emotional and conscious urges.

Ideally all three zones should be the same size, although this is rarely the case; neglect or exaggeration of one zone is usually to the detriment of the others. All three zones therefore need to be studied with great care.

To understand fully the interpretation of children's handwriting it is necessary to study first the handwriting of adults in order to establish the function of the three

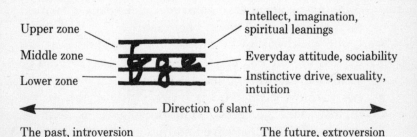

Upper zone — Intellect, imagination, spiritual leanings

Middle zone — Everyday attitude, sociability

Lower zone — Instinctive drive, sexuality, intuition

← ————————— Direction of slant ————————— →

The past, introversion   The future, extroversion

zones, which aren't always so apparent in children's writing. The following examples of adult handwriting explain the meaning of the three zones clearly.

THE UPPER ZONE

- Tall ascenders to the letters indicate a child who is striving too hard for perfection, or is perhaps too idealistic.
- Loops in the upper zone show quick emotional responses; the child is affectionate, and makes friends easily.
- Extremely large upper loops show an inflated ego – a child who shows off and continually seeks attention.
- Going over the upper loops two or three times shows insecurity, and can point to neurosis.
- Very small upper loops show a lack of emotion – the child may be very matter of fact.
- Very thin upper loops suggest little imagination, as well as little social warmth and affection.
- Confused and over-sized upper loops point to a muddled mind.

THE MIDDLE ZONE

The middle zone tells you whether the child is a thinking or a feeling personality.

- A script that is very large in the middle zone points to self-absorption, coupled with a friendly outgoing character.
- The script that is small in the middle zone indicates a thinking personality – someone who keeps a rein on their emotions and doesn't act rashly.
- Large handwriting in the middle zone points to an expansive nature; small handwriting in the middle zone to a reserved nature.
- An extremely regular, or even rigid, script in the middle zone suggests complusiveness, a fear of deviating from a perceived norm.

THE LOWER ZONE

It is in the lower zone that the subconscious impulses and urges are detected, the key letters to look at being the g, j and y, i.e. the letters with descenders. As the child develops, their emerging sexuality will be revealed in the lower zone.

This is a well-balanced handwriting script, with equal proportions in the three zones. Connected script shows a progressive movement towards an objective and systematic thinking, a practical application of energy and effort.

This script show exaggerated proportions in the middle zone. Too much emphasis is placed on the social aspect of life as the writer seeks to express her personality through this area. It is the pivot and symbolises the social and sentimental part of the mind, the adaptation to everyday reality.

This handwriting script is exaggerated in the lower zone – note the long descender.

This handwriting, with its tall ascenders, shows exaggeration in the upper zone. Expressing reflection and imagination linked with abstraction and speculation, when too tall and thin can reveal seeking after perfection and religious leanings.

4
THE BASIC FORMS OF HANDWRITING

There are four basic forms of handwriting:

- Angular
- Arcade
- Thread
- Garland

Each one has different characteristics, and must therefore be studied separately. When analysing a piece of handwriting all the traits have to be taken into consideration before a report is issued; no one trait in its own should be relied upon to form a pen picture of an individual.

ARCADE WRITING

Arcade writing is a formal style of handwriting. The arcade writer is often rather aloof from the outside world but adapts to it in his own special way. He has a need for form and behaviour – social and artistic. Many arcade

> . The fruit of the plant must be attractive usually it has a sweet taste and is of colour. The animals eat the fruit and

An example of arcade writing with good spacing.

writers direct their energies into creative spheres – music, painting, etc. Slow speed and carefully formed letters indicate the writer needs to be understood, he wants his writing to be clear and readable. There is a little immaturity in the rounded strokes but reliability and head control in the baseline and upright letters.

GARLAND WRITING

Garland writing flows along the page easily, often without pressure. Garland writers are receptive and less aggressive, more emotionally inclined. The rounded movement shows an open sociable character; they are impressionable and avoid conflict whenever possible.

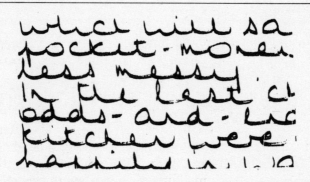

An example of garland script with a slight left slant. Slightly obsessive in its regularity, this writing denotes warmth and friendliness even though there is a left slant to it. The shallow garlands are broad and reveal generosity with a need for space, a conflict free environment and emotional sphere to function in.

THREAD WRITING

Thread writing tends to dwindle away into threadlike strokes. The thread writer is usually mentally agile, manipulative and ready for most situations. He is quick to adapt to changing circumstances, and has a tendency to grab opportunities. He is difficult to pin down to one course of action due to his versatility.

Thread writing with pasty script.

ANGULAR WRITING

In an angular script the lines are sharp, and sometimes even pointed. This differs from the other three formations as it is far more rigid and controlled.

The angular writer may have suffered from influences in the past preventing spontaneity. His disciplined writing impedes his speed as the movement doesn't allow for easy flow. There may be aggressive tendencies and head control rather than emotion. A very differentiating mind and critical sense. Nothing blurred – black/white, strong sense of duty and discrimination, poor tolerance level in the sharp script and pointed angles.

Angular writing with a right slant.

5
THE SLANT

As has been indicated in the samples on pages 23–5, the left or right slant to the writing indicates the degree of introversion or extroversion, respectively, of the writer.

Introverted children will be self-sufficient, and basically able to make their own decisions and employ their own judgment. Their powers of concentration are usually higher than those of the extrovert and they will always be cautious in their approach before planning any action. Because introverted children do not have the instant impulsive social attitude that extroverts have, they usually choose their close friends with discretion and aren't easily persuaded by other people's opinions. They need sympathy and understanding, but cannot be coerced into explaining their isolation or worry. Encouragement and support will help them to overcome any lack of confidence or shyness.

In contrast, extroverted children demand stimulation, action and plenty of company around them. They are socially minded little people who like to be independent; they thrive on enthusiasm, activity and the friendship of their peers. They may not be terribly consistent in their schoolwork or at home, but need to have their energies and talents directed into constructive channels so that they can assert themselves without fear of too many restrictions, which can cause rebelliousness. Because they are apt to act impulsively and without thought for the consequences, they can make a few mistakes.

The terms and conditions stated in correspondence are as we agreed and am happy to accept the position

An example of a basic left slant, indicating a character that is introspective, shy and reserved. The wide spaces often show caution, isolation and sometimes inhibition but also good organising and planning ability.

s colleague who informed me that you were logist.

in interested in having my hand writing so could you please inform me of the cost

This handwriting example demonstrates a left slant with a narrow script. It shows an introverted and inhibited character, due to an emotional blockage. It represents a desire for fundamentals, a lack of imagination and an obsessive need for uniformity of thought and action. The measured height and rhythm severely handicaps spontaneity.

training must be tailored to the times, products and market areas, in down and in house training has storing of performance and application

A handwriting sample showing thread writing with a left slant. The character is manipulative and intelligent, yet adaptable. The writer will adapt but at a cost *to definite character. Elusive and with a disregard for established forms and conventions, the writer is not firmly anchored in self.*

girl I was meant to stay with had cpectedly gone out so I really was in er a desperate position!

This is a classic upright script, with neither a left nor a right slant. It shows that the character is ruled by reason rather than emotion. In particular, upright writing in children demonstrates independence.

I refer to our discussion this afternoon and would be pleased to accept the position

This is a normal right slant. It demonstrates well balanced links with the outside world, indicating a character that is sociable and who looks to the future. There is speculation and thought for the future, altruism and social activity, recognition and regard for others.

Before the end of the North. the in own come

An example of handwriting with an exaggerated right slant. It shows an emotional impulsiveness and impatience; the individual has no resistance against outside influences. Is far too impressionable and

responsive to the influence of others due to too much dependency on the outside world through a lack of inner security and stability. Showing a strongly sensual nature, love of colour and some creativity. The spacing and baseline show organising skill and reliability but the heart often rules the head.

group, who amongst other things are in the production of a resource kit part of the personal development New South Wales schools. I also lesbian group a bit like the

This handwriting sample demonstrates a varying slant, indicating variations in mood and a conflict between the dominance of the mind and the emotions. Caused by mood variation this will cause the writer to be impressionable and easily irritated, particularly with outside influences. This can impair concentration resulting in a mercurial restlessness.

6
ALIGNMENT

Whether lined or unlined paper is used, the way the alignment of the handwriting is controlled is very important. Does the writing slope up or down the page, or does it go straight across?

STRAIGHT

A straight line, without any variation, is a sure sign of self-control and self-discipline, as evidenced by the ability to maintain consistency while writing. Attitude towards family and friends is likely to be reliable and straightforward.

However, your children, because they have a short focus of attention, usually find it hard to maintain a straight line when writing. This is something that is more likely to develop as the child gets older.

SLOPING UPWARDS

Does the baseline of the child's writing slope upwards? If so, it indicates enthusiasm, optimism and ambition. However an excessively sloping line can indicate over-excitement and haste; the child may be trying too hard to achieve their aims, such that their hopes and feelings run away from them.

SLOPING DOWNWARDS

If the baseline of the child's writing slopes downwards it shows pessimism and even depression. On a temporary basis a downward slope can show that the child is not happy with life at the time of writing – they are dissatisfied with themselves. A downward slope can also demonstrate a sensitive character, who can easily be hurt.

If a downward slope is coupled with weak writing pressure, it could be the result of fatigue. Perhaps the child is lacking in energy due to illness.

WAVY BASELINE

An undulating wavy baseline can be a sign of a versatile character. However it can also indicate inconsistent behaviour and an erratic mind that cannot concentrate on one thing for very long. The child may be impressionable, open to external influences and lacking a strong willpower.

There may be a touch of creativity that needs to be channelled into positive areas.

Today has all the elements of Spring

This handwriting sample has a rising slope to it, showing a tendency to optimism, ambition and enthusiasm. Although the left slant reveals reserve and discrimination the writer is introspective but friendly.

Today has all the elements of spring.

A handwriting sample with a descending slope to it. The writer has a tendency to pessimism and despondency, with a critical edge to their character. The erratic slant reveals an unpredictable nature, where impulsiveness fights with control causing conflict and subconscious uncertainty. This inner struggle results in indecision and inconsistency.

This is an example of my handwriting for analysis by your guest on the programme

This handwriting is nicely horizontal – a feature of a reliable character. It shows firmness, directness and self-control, plus reliability and firmness. The writer can maintain drive, will complete an undertaking and isn't easily distracted from his goal.

environment would be advantageous at this my career.

I am 29 yrs of age and have three years in Telesales initially as a cnvl

An undulating handwriting sample. This demonstrates an element of inconsistency in the character, and a lack of stability, together with an unsteady frame of mind. There is emotion discord in the fluctuating pressure and hyper-sensitivity in the sharp strokes which would manifest itself in touchiness and anxiety under pressure.

STACKING

Stacking refers to the way a child arranges the words on a sheet of paper, tending to line the words up vertically, one underneath another. The result is that the easy flow of words across the page is prevented or severely limited; the child appears to be more concerned with the vertical arrangement of words than in allowing them to run smoothly.

Stacking in a child's handwriting implies a character that is fearful of making mistakes, or apprehensive of someone who is causing them to feel isolated from their environment. The child feels very insecure, and if you try to question them in detail about the problem they are likely to clam up. For this reason, a lot of understanding, patience and skill are often needed to get to the root of the problem.

Normally stacking disappears after a short time – it is usually only a temporary phenomenon. However, if it persists, professional help may be needed in order to bring the child's anxiety to the surface and to deal with it.

This is a straightforward case of stacking, in which the words are lined up diagonally down the page. The lack of flow and rhythm in this sample of writing is a clear indication of the writer's emotions being blocked and reveals his inability to go forward without apprehension.

Sea monster has Shineing
that Shine up in the sea
body is made of Shineing
onds made you and me.
teeth are made of pures
So pretty he is; that is

This example of stacking in a child's handwriting suggests he has difficulty in coming to terms with his surroundings. He feels lonely and far from secure in his home environment and needs the re-assurance of love and affection from his loved ones.

han
th
l
yie there
my
l played
frund
we
played
and Seh then we
culas hous went to

In this handwriting sample, not only do we see evidence of stacking, but there is also a downwards slope to the writing line, suggesting depression. Although this writing is stacked it is also demonstrating a pessimistic attitude preventing the child from developing into a more positive little fellow.

7
SIZE OF HANDWRITING

The size of the child's handwriting tells you a lot about the child, for it is indicative of their social attitude – how they feel about their family and friends, and how they cope with the people around them. It also tells you a lot about their self-confidence.

There are basically three different sizes of handwriting: small, medium and large.

LARGE WRITING

Very large handwriting demonstrates a true extrovert – a child who loves to be the centre of attention, thriving on admiration. Such children like to show off and have a strong need for self-expression; they need to have lots of friends around them, and enjoy an active social life.

There may also be an element of vanity in their character, too, to the extent that they may be easily influenced by flattery.

SMALL WRITING

The child with small writing is quite the opposite to the large writer. They are the introverts, perhaps more interested in things than people. They may shun an active social life, although this doesn't mean that they don't need close friends, merely that they are more discriminating in their choice than the large writer.

There is a degree of introspection in the character of the small writer that will limit their showing-off and attention seeking. they may be cautious and reserved.

When the writing is particularly tiny and cramped it may indicate an inferiority complex.

MEDIUM WRITING

The majority of children will exhibit a medium-sized handwriting, showing a good balance between the mind and the emotions. Like all children, they will show off at times, at other times be quiet and reserved, but neither of these two facets of their personality will dominate.

Socially they will be able to mix comfortably, without being either reserved or over-familiar.

This is an example of an average-sized script, with no undue emphasis or exaggeration in any of the three zones. It shows a well-balanced intelligent character. The speed indicates intelligence and the ability to think quickly and consistently as the writer isn't going to waste time and effort on non-essentials.

This sample of handwriting is large, to an exaggerated degree. It demonstrates an egotistical streak in the character, very subjective and given to self-love. There are signs of considerable vanity and a strong desire for attention and admiration. The writer needs to express her personality and will do so with a great deal of show and ostentatiousness.

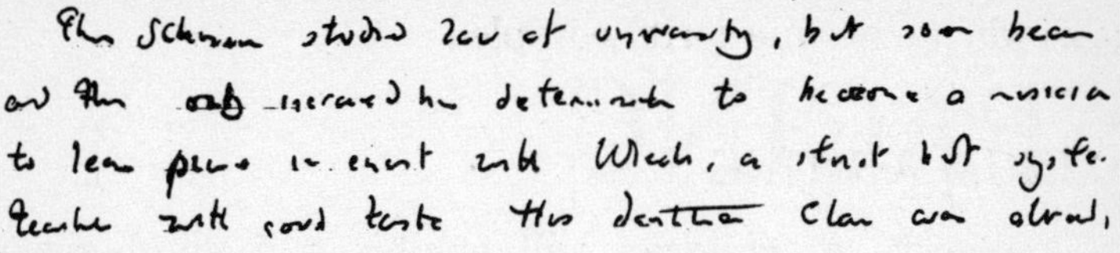

[handwritten sample]

This handwriting is small, indicating an intelligent individual – analytical and quick thinking. More inclined to channel his energies into assimilating facts and with an academic personality he will use intentional understatement. May occasionally be pedantic and can give way to over-scrupulousness.

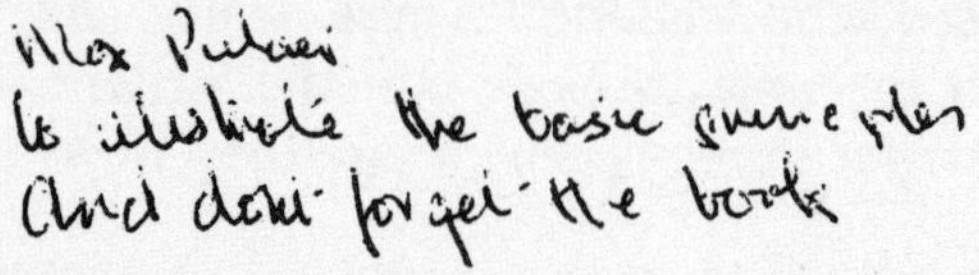

[handwritten sample]

An example of an over-small script. This demonstrates a character dominated by feelings of inferiority. The writer tends to be over-cautious, introverted and far too preoccupied with his own feelings and emotions. There is a fear of too much contact with the outside world.

8
SPACING

The spacing used in the handwriting – both between words and between lines – is very important.

SPACING BETWEEN WORDS

On a practical level, the spacing between words can be linked to the writer's organisational abilities. For example, are the spaces separating the words neat and tidy, or disorganised and chaotic? These traits can invariably been seen to carry through into the writer's thinking – does the writer think clearly, or are their ideas always in a muddle?

But the spacing between words can also be linked with the child's sociability. Wide spacing suggests a social cautiousness that may lead to isolation or loneliness, while close spacing could be indicative of a need for human company, perhaps on an unselective basis.

---

you to look into it for

sorry that there isn't

Here is an example of writing with large spaces between the words. It shows a cautious individual who is isolated socially.

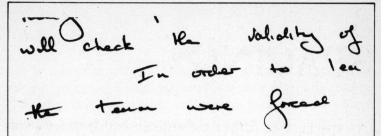

This handwriting sample exhibits over-large spaces between the words, indicating someone who is fearful of making mistakes. This will place a limit on the friendships they make, leading to loneliness.

Here we see very narrow spacing between the words; indeed some of the words almost seem to run together, indicating a rather chaotic muddle-headedness. Not a well organised individual.

An example of handwriting with average and equal spacing between the words. The writer has good organising abilities, a facility to think clearly. A cautious personality is also implied.

SPACING BETWEEN LINES

There are many parallels to be drawn from spacing between words and spacing between lines.

Of most importance, perhaps, the arrangement of the lines on the page gives a clue to the child's facility at organising. Evenly spaced lines will to show a well ordered child, confident in their organisational skills. Unevenly spaced lines arranged in a disorganised manner indicate much more erratic thinking, although this can be coupled with an imaginative spontaneity.

This is an example of my handwriting
I will be looking forward to hearing the

This example of handwriting demonstrates a clear and regular spacing between the lines, and implies a character that is both intelligent and well ordered. There is also evidence of quick writing, which indicates a rapid grasp of facts and situations.

When you write, would
kindly return the
? (The envelope got
the rain).

In contrast, the spacing between the lines in this script is very badly arranged. It reveals an individual who is indecisive, characterised by erratic thinking, even though the other features of the handwriting show a fertile and spontaneous mind.

9
CONNECTED AND DISCONNECTED WRITING

The ability of a child to connect up their writing will obviously depend on their age and maturity; for example, a child of 7 or 8 will have much less facility at connected writing than a child of 12 or 13. However, as handwriting ability develops, it will be noticed that some scripts will be more connected, and some more disconnected, than others.

In part this will reflect the speed of writing – the quicker the writing, the more fluent and continuous it will look. And speed of writing, in turn, tells you a lot about the character of the writer.

- For example, a very fast script indicates a bright child who perhaps has an ability to tackle essentials quickly and without any fuss.
- In contrast, a slow disconnected script may indicate a more cautious approach to life, especially where decisions are involved; perhaps even to the extent of missing out on opportunities because of a reluctance to take chances.

But the degree to which the writing is connected or disconnected also reveals a considerable amount of information about the child's facility at thinking – their ease at working out ideas and linking them together.

- An easily connected script shows a methodical thinker who will work things out in a continuous process until a satisfactory solution has been arrived at.

- In contrast, disconnected script indicates an erratic thinker – someone who might give up on an idea and switch to something else too easily.
- However, disconnected writing can also demonstrate an ability to come up with different ideas easily; an intuitive mind.

This is a good example of connected handwriting. It shows progressive movement and an easy flow; a writer who is able to develop a continuous process towards an objective. Someone who is a systematic thinker.

This is a typical disconnected script, belonging to someone with individualism. They are an 'ideas' person, with a well-developed sense of intuition and insight, although sometimes illogical in their thinking.

The new Press Complaints Commission is considering whether it can accept complaints about Sunday Sport

This sample of handwriting shows a mixture of connected and disconnected features, and implies an indecisive character. Their thinking allows for the germination of ideas, but only within a limited field.

10
PRESSURE IN HANDWRITING

When looking at handwriting scripts, the pressure that the writer exerts can tell you a lot about their vitality.

However, before conducting any sort of analysis, it is important to take into consideration the type of pen that is being used. A felt-tip pen, for example, may produce a script that appears to have been written with very heavy pressure, when in fact the writing is very light. It is therefore advisable to obtain a handwriting sample produced by a fountain pen or a ballpoint pen, as this will indicate the degree of pressure most accurately. And if you have any doubt about the amount of pressure used, examine the back of the page; if the indentation caused by the pen shows through the page, this demonstrates conclusively that heavy pressure has been used.

The degree of pressure used in writing will give an important clue to the amount of energy – the dynamic urge – the writer has. Is the child full of activity, perhaps with an emotional nature? Or are they much more sensitive, perhaps highly strung, with few reserves of energy to fall back on?

AVERAGE PRESSURE

As might be expected, medium pressure is used by the majority of people, and therefore tells of a balanced energy level. Other than that the writer has a good balance between emotion and mind, the heart and the head.

Instead you need to look closely at other features of the writing to gain an insight into the personality and character.

LIGHT PRESSURE

Light pressure can point to a bright and alert individual, although with a sensitive side to their character. Such a writer may well be susceptible to criticism, and is quickly offended.

The light pressure indicates an ability to write with the minimum expenditure of energy, but they can be very sarcastic and quick to argue when they feel they are right.

On a more practical level, weak writing could merely be a sign of poor health.

HEAVY PRESSURE

Heavy pressure shows someone who places plenty of emphasis on the physical; they will have plenty of drive, energy and enthusiasm, although at the extreme this can turn into aggression and a desire to have their own way, irrespective of the consequences. A heavy writer is likely to be an active person who gets things done. They will probably be forceful and dominating in discussions, and perhaps confrontational in arguments.

Heavy writing also carries the suggestion of egotism, stubborness, irritability and force.

This sample of handwriting with a heavy pressure indicates an individual with tenacity, energy and vitality. However, there is an element of aggression to them; they will be forceful in an argument.

ERRATIC PRESSURE

As might be expected, if the writer has an erratic writing pressure it indicates quickly changing moods, perhaps based on some sort of emotional disturbance, all conspiring to unsettle their overall self-control.

This example of a light script shows someone who is sensitive; they are susceptible to atmospheres, to moods and to people, which indicates an element of touchiness. They are lacking in vitality.

This is a typical example of a handwriting sample with average pressure, showing a satisfactory balance between the intellectual and the emotional sides of the character.

11
THE CAPITAL I

The formation of the capital I – the personal pronoun – is very revealing as it indicates how the child sees themselves. Do they value themselves? Do they have self-esteem? Or do they devalue their ego, and feel worthless? All this will be revealed by the formation of this one capital letter.

- A capital I that is a definite vertical straight line shows an intelligent child, quick thinking and practical. There is a good balance between the mind and the emotions.
- A tiny capital I indicates a lack of self-confidence, perhaps coupled with an inbuilt pessimism. The child may well have been repressed within the family.
- A very large capital I demonstrates a sense of self-importance – an egotistical nature, perhaps with a tendency to be the centre of attention and to show off.
- An I that is considerably larger or higher than the other capital letters suggests a child that is bossy, always wanting to dominate in games and other activities.
- A lean to the left is associated with the past, so an I that swings or leans to the left indicates the possibility of guilt based on a disappointment in the past, to the extent that it is now affecting the child's personality.
- In contrast, a capital I leaning to the right suggests an affectionate and socially outgoing child.
- A rounded or circle-like capital I suggests a sense of humour, and even a sense of the dramatic.
- An exaggerated loop to the I points to an emotional personality – warm and sentimental, but needing an equally warm and secure family life to depend on.
- A spiky angular I suggests a child that has been

thwarted and repressed, and who now may be sarcastic as a result.

- Loops to the I that roll together, tending to close the letter up, indicate someone who is trying to protect themselves from being hurt, who is afraid to open out and express themselves.

- An I that has two loops to it points even more to a personality that fears being hurt or damaged. There is a search for balance, coupled with a suspicion of other people's motives.

- A printed I shows an early creativity, linked as it is with the printed word. It can also demonstrate a desire for method and order in life.

- A complex I points to early self-awareness – an analytical brain, perhaps, coupled with a self-confident nature.

This capital I is a very definite vertical line, indicating an intelligent character and an ability to get down to essentials rapidly. Often shows leadership qualities and decisiveness, plus uncluttered thinking.

This handwriting sample shows a formal capital I, suggesting a familiarity with the printed word and an intelligent nature. Often found in the handwriting of people who are interested in literature, reading and the arts in general.

* is private*

ied. I am a

...an driving

In this script the I is very small – the same size as the other letters – and indicates an inferiority complex. Could be a hang-up from past emotional and environmental experiences which have left feelings of poor selfworth.

I wond

Can me

This rounded and curled I is a sign of a non-aggressive character. This is a defensive sign representing fear of outside influences penetrating the writer's 'safe' world of self.

I see

Here the capital I is wrapped around, collapsing in on itself. This suggests a fragile ego that is afraid of expressing itself.

12
INDICATIONS OF SEXUALITY

By examining a child's handwriting it is possible to gain some insight into their awakening sexual awareness, and find clues to any problems that might be developing.

THE IMPORTANCE OF THE LOWER ZONE

As we saw in Chapter 3, it is in the lower zone of the handwriting, i.e. the descenders of the letters, that the subconscious impulses and urges are detected. It is therefore this area of handwriting that can best reveal the child's attitude to sex and the manner in which they are coping – or not – with their developing sexuality.

The letters g, j and y are the important letters from this point of view, as they are the most frequently used letters with descenders. However, the letters f and q can also give useful clues in this respect, and the child may construct some other letters, particularly some capitals, with descenders.

ENROLLING

Enrolling of the descenders, i.e. the use of loops and curls, can be an indication that the child is placing too much emphasis on the physical instincts, to the extent that there may be a preoccupation with sex. And if the pressure on this enrolling is particularly heavy, it suggests that the child's emerging sexuality and sexual feelings are causing them discomfort and apprehension.

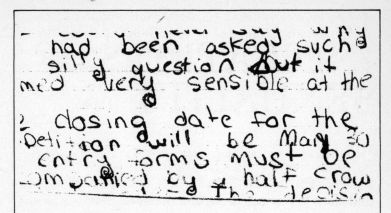

In this sample of a child's handwriting, the enrolling of the descenders is very marked, along with the use of heavy pressure specifically on the rolls and curls. Both suggest that the writer is having problems coming to terms with some aspect of their sexuality.

This piece of script also shows enrolling. Unlike the previous example, though, it is not so heavy, and is not on the descenders but on the rather elaborate capital letters.

HOMOSEXUALITY

Early signs of latent homosexuality in boys are evidenced by the descenders of the g and y tending towards the left, indicating a strong mother influence.

The early signs of lesbianism in girls are not so easy to spot in the handwriting. However, in the early teens it is possible to gain a clue to a girl's latent or apparent lesbianism by the appearance of a figure 8 in the descenders of the g and the y. This is often coupled with a left slant to the writing, revealing an opposition to the normal female role in society.

> The micro is usally set in BASIC so you can write programs and working's out also insteat of having a hole sun room for one computer you can have a screen a disk &drive and a keyboard instead of having a memory for large system

This sample of handwriting from a schoolboy shows the classic signs of latent homosexuality, in the leftward-tending loops of the g and y.

> to keep information on what houses they've solal and what are on sale. They are used for resonal diarys and computer games and booths. Musicians use them to write songs and to play them as well. when you use eletricity the electric metre

This is also the handwriting of a schoolboy, and again shows the loop of the descender – in this case the f and the g – tending towards the left. In both this and the previous case the boys were quiet and withdrawn in class.

not given

This is a sample of writing from a teenage girl. The figure-of-eight loop to the descender of the g points to the girl's lesbianism. The speed and small script all show her to be intelligent, socially minded and outward going.

my handwriting you can

Another piece of script from a teenage girl. This time her lesbianism is suggested more strongly, both by the 8 loop to the letter y and by the leftward slant of the writing.

13
EXAMPLES OF HANDWRITING ANALYSIS

In this chapter we will look at some average children's handwriting samples, and see what can be revealed by the application and interpretation of graphology.

YOUNGER CHILDREN

First let's look at some examples of handwriting from children in the 6 to 8 age range, beginning with two members of the royal family.

To Granny

for a very

merry Xmas

with all

love

from

Edward.

Prince Edward, aged 6, has writing that is barely joined up. There is a slight left slant, indicating shyness, and the uncertain pressure demonstrates his difficulty with the discipline of writing.

Prince William, aged 8, has a big bold signature, showing confidence and self-assurance. The underlining is an ego sign, symbolising the importance of his name, while the tall letters also indicate an awareness of his importance. He is a boy who knows what he wants and goes after it; the slightly angular lines and upright writing show he can be stubborn – he likes his own way. The pressure is firm, revealing plenty of energy and drive. The dot at the end of his name is an inhibitive signal, showing decisiveness. The open small a gives away his talkativeness at times. This is a mature signature for an 8 year old.

Describe fully the many ways in which a microcomputer is used today.
A microcomputer is used on games and writing stores. The microcomputer is used in schools too. They are usesullely used on maths and work like that. The microcomputer is a small computer. The computer has got a cursor. It's also has got a ROM and a RAM. The computer you joistick is used for games on the

Tom has small fast writing with excellent spacing. The speed of the script shows a slight inferiority complex, but the rightwards slant indicates a socially minded attitude.

A way to use a computer is that you can rigt a leter out
and ~~you alter~~ and all you thave got to dow is one
tuch ove a ~~~~ buton. And you can allsw play games you can
yoows a disk or a tap but the best fing to yoows is a disk.

Ronnie hasn't grasped the basics of spelling yet, and is
inclined to leave letters out. However, the upright
script suggests an independent character, while the
tidy spacing points to an organised and tidy thinker.

and etc. Computers are in lots of shapes and
sizes computers are used for ~~schools~~ enithing
and enine. Computers are a great
deal of work for you and me these
days computers are changed a 'little
bit ~~and~~ it has have a new memory
in it. Commyputers are usfull to uorself

Jason shows intelligence and speed in his handwriting;
for his age, he forms his letters with maturity. The
slant to his writing is variable but basically is directed
towards the right, suggesting friendliness. The angles
in his script suggest an element of firmness.

ou can play heman . and others.
If you were learning words you.
an do testing if your mum or
ad had to teach you.
ords they could Just say to
ou to look at the to thy
nd spell it.

Patrick is not going to co-operate; he seeks to be different and wants to do his own thing. The disconnected script points to a difficulty both in sticking to a routine and in following orders. He wants to be independent, yet the light pressure of the handwriting shows how sensitive he is.

One day I went to the Zoo.
I Saw Birds. Elephants. Lions.
Tigers. Lepords. Flemingo's. Horse's.
Zebra. Lizard. I bought some
Sweets. I had Lunch in the
Coach. I Went back to school.
By Nicola pullen

Bold, firm and well spaced and confident, Nicola has leadership qualities in her legible and upright handwriting. She is proud of her name and there is considerable assurance in the formation of her letters and the straight baseline.

Ann has excellent writing for an 8 year old. She reveals a lot of energy in her script, with her firmly made letters and rounded strokes. The slightly rising line of her writing shows her basic optimism, although the very slight leftwards slant indicates an initial shyness and reserve. She is an affectionate child, with good colour sense, and the fullness of her small letters shows she has some creative ability.

OLDER CHILDREN

Here are some more examples of handwriting, showing how graphology can detect the developing complexity of character as children grow older.

Christopher, 12, is familiar with spelling, and his writing is quite mature for his age; it races across the page, displaying his outward-going nature and desire to mix and communicate.

Other micros have ... ... than normal Computing, ... to store their ... ... Hospitals Use microcomp... to keep records and ... ...

Lawrence is intelligent, as shown by his ability to use the space on the page well, while his light pressure demonstrates a critical sense. The rhythm of his writing isn't particularly consistent, but he does show a touch of originality in his capitals and loops.

computers can be used off offices and paint shops and many other things too. Some people uses them as work computers thar are many microcomputers in the wold today, some people have them in banks the computers in the bank are very, very big a the people who operat them have to

Peter's parents are separated, so he lives with his mother. This has inevitably made its mark on his character – for instance, he doesn't make friends easily – and this can be seen in some features of his handwriting. For example, the cramped script with its long t bars shows an obstinate nature, added to which he is inhibited and inclined to be spiteful. The mixture of angles and arcades and variations in pressure show how his moods come and go, while the fluctuating slant shows how he is pulled emotionally in several directions at once.

> The quick brown fox jumps over
> the lazy dog,
>
> Jane Garnett.

Jane's writing is mature and well formed; it shows intelligence, mental agility and firmness. There is a combination of logic and intuition in the spacing between the letters, while the Greek e indicates a familiarity with the printed word. She has an excellent eye for detail, is sociable and able to mix and communicate with skill. She is forward looking, as evidenced by the rightwards slant to her script, and has a strong need to express her personality. An independent character who is going to be strong willed and confident, she would do well to channel her energies and ideas into writing and communicating.

14
CHILDREN WITH
PROBLEMS

In this last chapter of this section we will look at the handwriting of children with various problems, and see how graphology can help us gain clearer understanding of what their problems are and where these problems stem from.

> Theis two pags give you some
> print practice using the commad
> Those

Christopher, aged 6, is a highly nervous child, unstable in his reactions, who constantly demands attention in class. He finds it hard to adapt to any environment. His writing is messy and untidy, with unevenly formed letters and varying sizes; the over-stroking of his script is a neurotic sign. The mingling lines indicate his inability to maintain any discipline, while the irregular pressure shows that emotional conflict is interfering with his mental stability. The long underlengths of his g and y reveal imagination, but also strong urges in the subconscious instinctual area.

computers on & so you with ✗

beaboo to do Safi. fithik and if

you wot to play a gam poot **LOAD**

then it wrth LoAD In srep you inen

mne tuls.

Raymond, age 7, is under pressure at home from a dominant father who wants him to achieve; consequently Raymond feels insecure and unhappy as he tries to live up to his father's expectations. The symbolic filling in of the word 'Load' reveals the tension the boy is under. The wide spacing between his words shows he feels isolated, while the rather shaky letters are a sign of his nervousness.

And it can do thager for you.

And the secand computers had a

little bet of memvey

and it can do priir

wat later you wath

And It can do

ofen tege for you.

And It will do every trige

For you.

Jason, age 8, has stacked his words one above the other – a sign of anxiety and insecurity. He has caring parents and comes from a good home, but is nervous and afraid of his environment. Mischievous in school and anxious, he needs counselling to direct his fears away from his surroundings. Stacking is frequently found in the hand-writing of children who leave their original country, or who have been placed in an alient environment and so feel insecure.

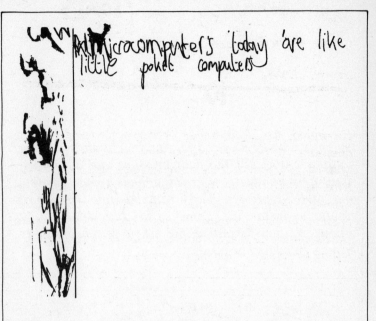

Harry, age 10, digs his pen in so hard on the paper that he makes holes. This lack of coordination, and the overlapping lines, both show his poor emotional control. He is nervous, easily excited and unsettled in school, quickly becomes irritated and makes no effort; a very unresponsive child, he displays many angry angles in his script. His frustration needs to be directed outwards before he becomes even more angry.

Here is a sample of my
writing for your programme
of Thursday.

From Nigel.

age 11

Not only does Nigel, aged 11, find it difficult to stay on
a straight line, but the light pressure and downward
slope of his handwriting show that he is hyper-sensitive
and mildly depressed. The erratic baseline is a sign of
emotional instability. Some of his letters are quite
original in their formation, but his rhythm is unsteady
as he is ruled by his moods.

to see a birds ...

and PLANTS and Insects
and MAMMALS

2.   you —Some ANIMALS
     EAT other ANIMALS

3.   Some ANIMALS Eat BoT

4

Charles, the product of a broken home and an
unsettled lifestyle with his mother, is on the welfare list
of at-risk children. Very disruptive in class, and often
inviting trouble, he creates scenes. His large writing,
angular script and the erratic rhythm all point to his

restlessness. The spiky strokes suggest a lot of pent-up aggression, which, if not channelled into action and positive spheres, could erupt into violence.

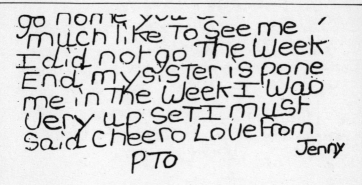

go nom... you ...
much like To See me
I did not go The Week
End my sister is pone
me in The Week I Wao
Very up SeTI musr
Said cheero LoveFrom
Jenny
PTO

This copybook handwriting without any originality was written by a 13 year old girl in care. She came from a broken home, was difficult to handle and yet from the rounded script she is affectionate and needs love. The lack of spacing between words and lines reveals her need for human contact, but the upright letters and size of her capitals indicate feelings of inferiority and diffi-culty in letting go her emotions. When she writes her name she squeezes it in at the bottom almost apologeti-cally.

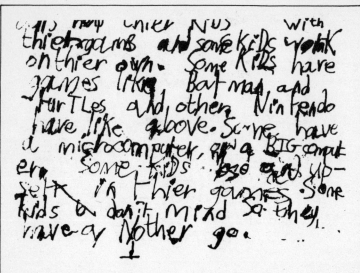

Terry's messy and poorly formed script, with its smudges and mistakes, reveals hyper-activity and a considerable amount of wasted energy in the pressure. The heavy i dots indicate tension. Terry has little idea of discipline; he is unable to distinguish between the lines, and is muddled and confused when it comes to spacing. He has caring and affectionate parents, but is very disturbed in the emotional sphere and can't settle to any kind of routine at school because his emotions are too intense for him to cope with.

there was an old lady of ninety two

there was an old lady of ninety two, died
the foo inkie pinkie parlevoo.

2 Fart went rolling down the street
Fart went ↗ ↗ ↗ ↗ street
Fart went ↗ ↗ ↗ ↗ and
inkie junkie parlevoo.

3 Copper got out his rusty pistol 1
↗ ↗ ↗ ↗ ↗ ↗

An unusual way of demonstrating hostility and anger is seen in this writing, with its arrows underneath the words. The fluctuating baseline and erratic writing, plus the downward slope, all provide a pen portrait of a very tense young man who badly needs to release some of the pressure he's under. His considerable energy should be channelled into constructive spheres where he can use his initiative without too many restrictions being imposed on him, but where there is enough discipline to keep him from lashing out at the world in general.

The wide spacing between letters and varying slant tell of moodiness and inconsistency. By crossing his name underneath – a graphological symbol of anxiety in a child's signature – David is saying that he is not happy, that he could be feeling stressed. (Occasionally this sign has been seen when suicidal feelings are lurking in the unconscious.) David needs to be encouraged to talk over his difficulties, to discover the reason for his unhappiness.

ive the eodings ta a omputer. as cau Typ say ——
a omputer to hect the Preure ox the oil ow.
Polis .ise t i rean aor eye on ohere thier cars are
grien . omputer are used to control Robots and
mad to matee Sure that generators run smoothly.
Faeyace

Malcolm, age 13, has an unsettled home life. His father is away most of the time, and he lives with his mother and two brothers; but his mother is indifferent to the child, who is withdrawn and quiet in school. Malcolm's writing reveals latent homosexual tendencies in the left swing of the underlengths of his small g and y. The *upright slant shows his lack of emotion; he desperately seeks affection and love, seen in the small spacing and slightly pasty writing.*

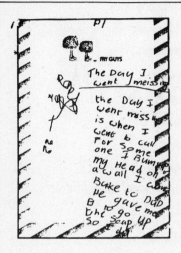 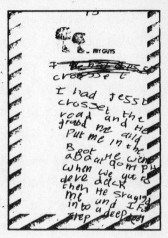

This childish scribble, written by a 7 year old girl who was abducted, strangled and left for dead by her assailant, shows clearly the depression she is suffering months after the attack. The downward lines reveal her attitude of unhappiness, although she manages to put a brave face on her ordeal. The clarity of her detail is astonishing for a child of her age. This letter was written entirely at her own instigation; hopefully by bringing out into the open the dreadful occurrence she will not suffer traumatic effects later.

Vous aimez le tennis?
Vous aimez le rugby?
Vous aimez les choux à la crème?
Vous aimez la monopolie?
Vous aimez les mots croisés
Vous aimez le basket?
Vous aimez le métro?
Vous aimez les puces?
Vous aimez les jeunes filles?
Vous aimez la musique "Pop"?
Vous aimez le cinéma?
Vous aimez la radio?
Vous aimez les animaux?
Vous aimez la campagne?
Vous aimez londres?
Vous aimez les autobus?
Vous aimez les avions
Vous aimez les greves
Vous aimez les autos
Vous aimez les bijoux

This excessively compulsive writing, with its rigid conformity, belongs to a 14-year-old girl who lived with elderly parents who were exacting and achievement-motivated; although kind and considerate, they pushed her hard to do well at school. There is, perhaps not surprisingly, a lot of repression indicated in this script. It lacks flow and release, and is full of tension; the

*writer needs to relax and allow her emotions more
outlet. The heavy pressure confirms that she is over-
controlled, so that each action she performs – including
her writing – is compulsive.*

> parents when they are wrong and ...
> them they are going to experience a lot of difficulties
> and hardships and if the parents don't listen to the
> teenagers when they are wrong they are going to have a
> lot of resentment from the teenagers.
> Also I think that it's okay for a parent to be strict so
> long as he or she don't be over-strict because they
> could loose feeling for the teenagers and could make
> them feel that they have no freedom.
> So the teenagers and parents should try to talk things
> over and see who is right; admit to being wrong when
> they are; and, understand eachother. Teenagers
> should take parents advice when they know they are right
> and be ready to admit to being wrong when they are
> also they should be understanding and not resentful
> Parents shouldn't be over strict and should make the

*Rigid and close together, this writing signifies a great
deal of apprehension. The lack of spacing between
words and lines shows a neurotic need for security. It
reveals an unsure ego and craving for contact and yet
an inability to see things or people clearly.*

we use them for working things out
like sums for insthomes and
like how much cars way, and
that thats the way we use computers
or computers today. and we them for
diarys use them for diary arias as well
today, now we usese. computers for
games as well as Hard writing.

*James, age 13, comes from a broken home, lives with
his mother and is on the welfare at-risk register. He is a
problem child at school. His writing is unstable and
lacking in any consistency. He finds it hard to
concentrate, and the erratic pressure shows sudden
bursts of temper; he has a limited focus of attention,
and badly needs discipline in his life. The angular
strokes demonstrate his anger, and the crossings-out
his nervousness and insecurity. He feels that, being
deprived of security, he can do what he likes.*

This slow copybook writing belongs to a female offender, age 16, a young girl who is unable to express her personality except through hostility to authority. The heavy filling in of letters, the thick strokes and heavy dot above the i show her depression and sadness. In youth custody for various crimes, she is against all the people who try to help her, and rebels as a protest against her own unhappiness; yet she can be quite kind and sympathetic to other inmates until she is thwarted.

ANALYSING CHILDREN'S PICTURES

Unfortunately there is very little evidence of children's drawings having been saved from the past. This may possibly be due to the fact that paper and pens were expensive and exclusively the tools of the rich; or perhaps it was because children were not considered particularly important enough to warrant a lot of attention, until a couple of hundred years ago when children's education became of interest to the reformers.

Now, fortunately, the significance of children's drawings and paintings has been accepted, for they are seen as an expressive creation of the child's development and as such they are recognised as providing a valuable insight into the child's developing personality.

The chapters that follow outline the guidelines that need to be used when analysing children's drawings, before going on to examine some examples.

15
WHAT TO LOOK FOR

It was Carl Jung who first stressed the importance of signs and symbols, and explained how they can reveal clues to the individual's unconscious. Over the years this realisation has spawned a branch of psychology known as analytical drawing psychology, whereby the conscious features, figures and formations represented in a child's drawing are analysed to reveal the unconscious thoughts, emotions and feelings that lie beneath the surface, in order to bring out the hidden and secret hopes, fears, anxieties and stresses that are submerged. Used in this way, spontaneous picture interpretation can be as effective as dream interpretation. And it is something that the laymen can practise, provided they are aware of, and apply, the basic rules and guidelines. Once mastered, this form of analysis can give an absorbing and instructive insight into the minds of normal children, and opens valuable windows on the minds of those children with behaviour problems.

WHERE TO BEGIN

If you want to analyse your child's drawings provide him or her with plenty of paper and a choice of coloured pens, suggest a theme or subject and leave. Then you can leave it to the child's imagination to carry out the drawing without too much attention while he is busy. Never make them hurry their work; let them make their own speed.

Once the drawing is finished and you come to look at it, be as objective as you can without being too emotionally biased. And don't just look at one or two items but study the whole drawing to see what form has been used. For example:

- How much space does the picture take up on the page?
- Does it cling to the left of the page or to the right?
- Is the drawing bang in the middle?
- Are the figures and objects filled in?
- Does the child place the human figures alone or in groups?
- Are the figures carefully drawn or distorted?
- Does one figure loom larger than the others?
- Is there shading or stacking?
- Are the features angry, smiling or grotesque?
- Does the child include all the features – eyes, nose, mouth, etc.?
- Are things and people drawn out of proportion, or with exaggeration?
- Are the things and people angular or rounded?
- Are they small and cramped?
- Does the child edge the drawing?

All these answers will give clues to the child's personality, and unravel the mystery of characteristics hidden in his scribbles. But always remember that you are not seeking a full analysis of the child's character, personality and problems, merely a guide which will enable you to understand their thoughts and feelings a little better.

OVERHEAD LINES

Watch out for a heavy line, or lines, above the drawing, as this can point to a fear of something the child feels is hanging over him; for example, it can be a sign that all is not well within the family, and the child is apprehensive. However, this does not apply when the line is part of the drawing – the sky for instance.

MOVEMENT

Movement in drawings can take the form of figures running, jumping and walking, or animals that appear to be moving. Alternatively, the illustration might be lively and indicative of spontaneous actions and reactions.

TREES

Drawings of trees have long been seen as important by many psychologists, who use them to reveal patients' personalities. Although they may only give a brief insight into character, such drawings are amazingly accurate, and the conclusions drawn from a study of both crown and trunk can be extremely useful.

EDGING

Edging, as seen in the accompanying drawing, is where a child spreads his drawings round the edge of the page and leaves the middle clear. It reveals a fear of venturing too far from known and familiar things and people – home, parents, environment. The child boxes himself in to feel safe.

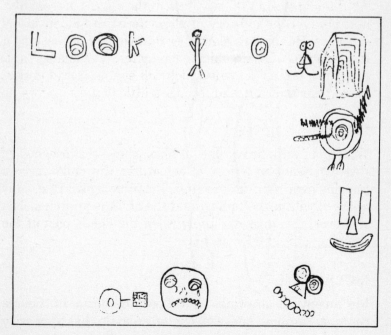

When this particular trait is apparent, the child may be need to be coaxed out of his self-imposed shell with sympathetic handling.

SEX

A preoccupation with sex, or mere sexual curiosity, in very young children can emerge in the form of drawings of female form, or of organs in male drawings. Or perhaps there might be a 'wish fulfilment' picture of a female face with flowing hair and beautiful features in teenage girls.

FIGHTING SPIRIT

Upraised arms represent anger in children's drawings, or pent-up feelings of frustration.

The accompanying drawing, with its large muscles and closed and barred fists, was drawn by a young man who was into body building and who was unhappy in his choice of career. He saw himself as being all powerful and in charge of his life, while the closed mouth indicates his inability to express his feelings at times.

16
YOUNGER CHILDREN'S DRAWINGS

In this chapter we will look at some typical features of drawings produced by young children.

Clinging to the top of the page, Allen's drawing shows he's a daydreamer. He also reverses his letters, displaying a poor focus of attention. He is easily distracted by external influences, for his strokes are not well developed or firm. There are many angles and squares in his drawing, and the grills represent feelings of being trapped.

Graham

Young Graham is tender-hearted and sensitive, as shown by his use of the bottom and middle of the page for his drawing; he doesn't like discord or friction, and there's a whimsical touch to his animal faces. His pressure is light – a sign of impressionability.

Most of David's drawing is to the right of the page, disclosing a forward-looking child who is active and energetic. For a five year old he has a good balance between mind and emotion, as shown by the smiling cat and well-drawn house. He still has a little difficulty with forming his letters – he tends to go over some of them – but this isn't too serious at his age.

Clinging to the left of the page, Jenny's drawing shows she is introspective and shy; she finds it hard to make friends, and needs lots of assurance from her family. Yet her drawing is full of activity and action; her lines are clearly and firmly penned and she is confident of her name. However the cramming together of the objects betray her insecurity. An intelligent imaginative five year old.

Robert

Robert has no qualms about letting his drawing take up all the space available. He is active, lively and has a sense of fun as shown by his well-drawn sun, circles and objects. Not for Robert to be hiding in a corner; he is an extroverted little boy who enjoys being in the centre of things. He's confident, well adjusted, and mixing and meeting with his peers holds no fears.

Shaun.D

Shaun, aged 5, is slightly aggressive in his attitude, his objects being precise, and more angled than round. Apart from the shading, he also applies considerable pressure, a sign that his feelings are quite intense at times. Many of his objects are drawn facing left – always an introverted sign.

Shirley is an extrovert, and socially minded, even though she underlines and boxes her name in – a cautionary factor. Her rounded strokes show her to be a loving and happy child who feels secure and loved. She chooses to draw animals and plants, symbolising a less intense and aggressive need to express herself. Her use of space is excellent.

Paul, aged 5, is quite an aggressive young man for his age. The figure he has drawn is full of angles, including the arms and hands. This means that there's more than a hint of resistance to authority, the squares and lines, rather than rounded strokes, revealing him to be argumentative and very sure of himself. He is strong willed, knows what he wants and usually gets it. The smiling faces, however, show a sense of fun.

Carl's stick-like figures, with their pointed hats and thin strokes, are without faces; although he does manage to convey action in their movement, they are faceless and without features. He isn't terribly happy at the time of scribbling them.

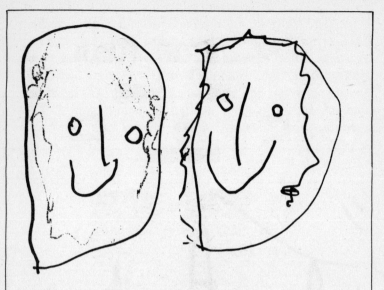

Emily, aged 4 years 4 months, is clever at forming her faces — she uses her drawing ability with skill. The smiling faces with their wide mouths, eyes, hair and noses show attention to detail, and she also uses all the space available to her. The firm vertical line in the middle of each face indicates that her intelligence is higher than average for her age group. She is a happy, contented and active little girl, friendly and bright, who feels secure, loved and wanted.

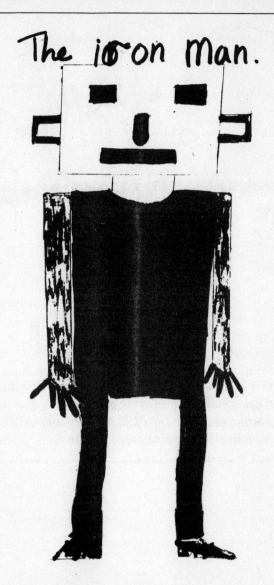

The iron Man.

In this drawing of the Iron Man there is a lot of detail in the hands and the formation of the feet – the drawing shows good powers of observation and an eye for detail. The lines are also firm and well drawn.

There is a lot of action indicated in this drawing; the plane has smoke coming out of the back, the child is riding a bicycle, even the little girl is laughing. This is a happy picture, with plenty of action in it.

These cleverly drawn birds show some skill in their execution – a colourful display of artistic awareness and detail. The fact that they face left represents a turning away on the part of the artist.

Tricia has added a multi-coloured roof to her house, and the little figure with its smiling face shows that she is happy to enter it. The chimney pot with its smoke has been added as afterthought, but the whole drawing shows a lively imagination.

The S bend in Alan's path leading to his house signifies intelligence, while the use of all the space on the page is a desire for freedom of expression and movement. The car in the garage and wide road with cats' eyes shows his sense of detail, while the fact that the road leads to the right shows forward thinking. Alan is obviously intelligent, energetic and observant; however the heavily filled-in roof to the house is a sign of mild emotional problems bothering him.

Paul, age 10, is a thinker who likes to delve into things and problems, albeit a worrier who is inclined to be easily distracted. He places his tree on an island, showing a need for security – he doesn't always feel happy with his peers, and doesn't make friends easily. He needs to 'belong' in his family circle, and is wary of outsiders. As he gets older he will channel a lot of his mental and physical energy into constructive rather than physical outlets; he should develop a practical streak. The highly original crown of his tree, with its spiky branches, represents a critical sense, and some inner aggression.

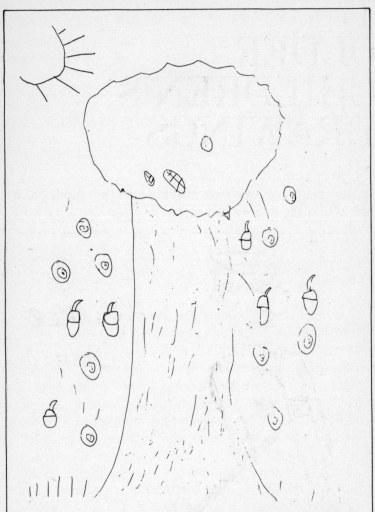

Andrew, age 8, is a feeling child with an affectionate nature and good social sense. The thick tree trunk in his drawing shows self-confidence, although the slightly smaller crown to the tree means he is a little shy. His use of space available demonstrates his need to be in the middle of things. The falling acorns reveal an active imagination; there is originality in this drawing, with suggestions of leadership qualities.

17
OLDER CHILDREN'S DRAWINGS

In this chapter we will look at some drawings produced by older children, mainly teenagers.

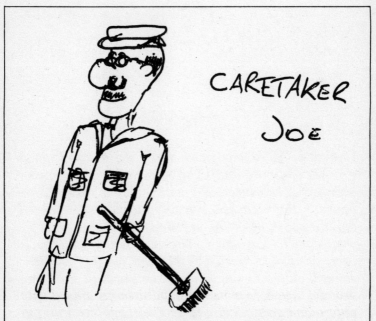

CARETAKER
JOE

Guy, aged 15, has an excellent eye for detail in his picture of Caretaker Joe; he gives him glasses, a moustache, mouth, tie, pockets, and a well-shaped broom. All this reveals Guy to be observant and aware of the significant features he sees; he has spent time and effort to notice quite a lot before attempting to draw Joe.

Charlotte

Charlotte, age 12, has drawn a tree, the crown of which consists of firmly and tightly drawn circles, showing her strong willpower and determination. By adding hands to the branches, instead of leaves, she shows a fighting spirit, while the upraised arms suggest aggression. Socially adaptable, but very self-willed, she is sometimes unresponsive to the pleas of other people – she will always try to do what she wants to do. There are also signs of emotional impulsiveness, tinged with self confidence, that could lead her into spontaneous action that isn't always harmonious.

Carol, age 14, has produced a drawing that has been quickly scribbled, indicating intelligence, but the placing of her tree on a slope is a sign of mistrustfulness. The fluffy crown is a little over-stroked – a tinge of nervousness – and it veers over to the right, indicating a need for social contact. Carol isn't a particularly confident youngster.

Bernie, age 17, has drawn a tree that has a series of dashes and lines for the crown, revealing inhibition and a tendency to withdraw and keep the world at bay. He has an off-beat sense of humour, and is highly sensitive and critical, compensating for this by assuming an indifferent attitude to those who try to probe his feelings. The trunk, with its dash-like strokes, tells of conflict in his early and formative years.

JONATHAN

Jonathan, age 16, has produced a drawing that contains more than a hint of artistic talent. The strong trunk is a sign of a practical and realistic approach to problems. The crown shows he is inclined to be disappointed and aggressive. The curiously shaped branches inside his tree indicate hidden fears and apprehensions that he doesn't seem to be able to resolve; he finds it difficult to discuss his inner feelings and hopes, and a lot of emotion is repressed. The shading of his tree and the varying direction of the branches show motivation is missing, while the roots demonstrate his insecurity.

Clare, age 14, has drawn a round fluffy crown to her tree, showing her passive nature, while the wide base of her tree trunk signifies her need for solid security, and the tiny bird-like dashes point to an excitable impulsiveness in her emotional responses. She is a particularly loving child, with a slightly gullible disposition, vulnerable in her need for affection. A somewhat immature 14 year old.

My name is Aaron Cant.
i'm 15 years old.
This is a tree
with birds
approaching it,
from the distant
clouds.

Aaron, age 15, has drawn a tree that is dark and forbidding, with a sense of brooding in the filled-in crown; it shows a strong willpower. The scar on the trunk is an unusual feature in a child's drawing, and reveals an unconscious trauma in his early years which has influenced him. His writing, combined with the drawing, demonstrates good head control, firmness and a sense of the dramatic.

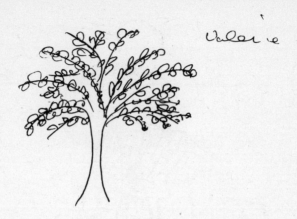

Valerie has drawn a tree with a long thin trunk, revealing considerable self-confidence and enthusiasm for new ideas, but also a longing for some inner fulfilment. The tiny ball-like leaves demonstrate the ability to keep a secret. Sociable, able to mix and communicate, but with caution before commitment, she may puzzle people with her motivations for some of her actions.

There is imagination in this house built on stilts, revealing many cautionary factors in the writer's personality. The well-drawn roof demonstrates an attention to detail and his ability to focus on a wide range of interests. There are more lines and angles than rounded strokes, indicating control, and the fluffy clouds confirm an imaginative personality. The clouds and sun show his basically optimistic nature, but there is distrust in the slope he places his building on.

18
CHILDREN WITH PROBLEMS

In this final chapter on analysing children's drawings we will look at some drawings produced by children who had readily identifiable problems, and see how these problems are expressed in their pictures.

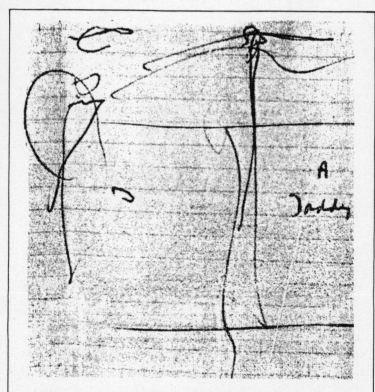

In 1968 a young girl called Maria Caldwell was brutally killed by her stepfather. However, some months before this occurred, she drew a picture of a

'father'. This drawing, with its stark bare lines and complete lack of curves or softening strokes, is a clear and graphic example of a drawing produced by a child starved of love and affection. The poverty of care is seen in the faces without features, the meagre thin bodies and the lack of proper limbs.

Philip effectively comes from a one-parent family; he lives with his mother, as his father was murdered. In this picture Philip has drawn himself at the side of his mother, who stands with upraised arms in a familiar attitude of angry frustration. He has drawn a tree high up on the page, showing that he does occasionally daydream; however the wavy lines lurking in the tree trunk reveal tiny fears. Philip's house is drawn slightly to the right of the page, showing him to be forward looking, but the windows appear to look to the left – a sign of his introspective nature.

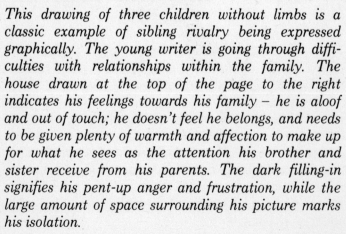

This drawing of three children without limbs is a classic example of sibling rivalry being expressed graphically. The young writer is going through difficulties with relationships within the family. The house drawn at the top of the page to the right indicates his feelings towards his family – he is aloof and out of touch; he doesn't feel he belongs, and needs to be given plenty of warmth and affection to make up for what he sees as the attention his brother and sister receive from his parents. The dark filling-in signifies his pent-up anger and frustration, while the large amount of space surrounding his picture marks his isolation.

This example of a drawing demonstrating sibling rivalry is by a young man who resented his cousin; his cousin was not only cleverer than him, but had a habit of boasting about it, with the result that the artist felt inferior.

Another example of sibling rivalry showing up in a drawing. This time the picture is by a young girl whose mother remarried. The man she married already had a young daughter, and the girl intensely disliked her new step-sister, as shown by the body with no limbs. The girl has become withdrawn and mildly aggressive in a bid for attention.

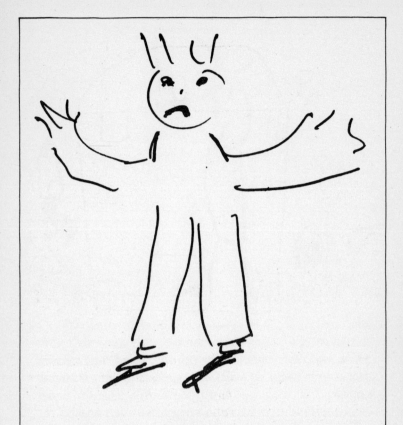

Arms upraised, an angry expression on the face, exemplified by the turned-down mouth, and a fierce stance, all combine to illustrate aggression. And as if that was not enough, the spiky strokes further emphasise the anger this picture generates.

Stark and bare, with smoke coming out of the chimney downwards, this drawing suggests that whoever produced it isn't too happy with life. His faces are drawn without features and are overstroked around the edges – a nervous sign. The father on the left is going away from the family, while the mother is alienated from the group. His sister is the only one he has attempted to give features to.

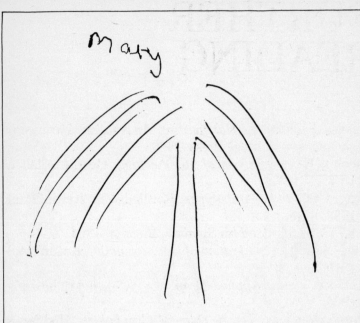

Mary's poor little weeping willow tree, with its sagging branches and long thin trunk, is evidence of her depression and loneliness; it shows her to be shy, withdrawn and bad at making friends, and reflects quite a lot of unhappiness. Her ego badly needs a boost; she requires reassurance from her family, and needs to be made to feel that she is important.

FURTHER READING

Hearns, Rudolph S., *Handwriting, An Analysis Through its Symbolism*, Vantage Press, 1966.

Jacoby, H.J., *Analysis of Handwriting*, George Allen & Unwin, 1939.

Jung, Carl, *Four Archetypes*, Routledge & Kegan Paul, 1959.

Jung, Carl, *Man and his Symbols*, Picador, 1964.

Jung, Carl, *The Integration of the Personality*, Kegan Paul, 1940.

Marcuse, Irene, *Applied Graphology*, Macoy Publishing, 1960.

Marne, Patricia, *Teach Yourself Graphology*, Hodder & Stoughton, 1980.

Marne, Patricia, *How To Analyse Your Handwriting*, Macdonald Optima, 1991

Mendel, Alfred O., *Personality in Handwriting*, Stephen Days Press, 1974.

Meyer, Oscar, *The Language of Handwriting*, Peter Owen, 1960.

Olanova, Nadya, *The Psychology of Handwriting*, Wiltshire, 1960.

Olanova, Nadya, *Handwriting Tells*, Peter Owen, 1978.

Roman, Klara, *Handwriting, A Key to Personality*, Routledge & Kegan Paul, 1954.

Saudek, Robert, *The Psychology of Handwriting*, George Allen, 1925.

Saudek, Robert, *Anonymous Letters*, Methuen, 1933.

Saudek, Robert, *What your Handwriting Shows*, T. Warner Laurie, 1932.

Singer, Eric, *A Manual of Graphology*, Duckworth, 1969.

Singer, Eric, *Personality in Handwriting*, Duckworth, 1974.

Sonnermann, Ulrich, *Handwriting Analysis*, Grune & Stratton, 1950.
Wolff, Werner, *Diagrams of the Unconscious*, Grune & Stratton, 1950.

FURTHER INFORMATION

If you want to find out more about graphology in general, contact:

The Secretary
The Graphology Society
33 Bonningtons
Thriftwood
Hutton
Brentwood
Essex CM13 2TL